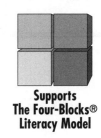

Poems for Shared Reading

by
Karen Sharpe

Editor
Joey Bland

Cover Design
Jennifer Collins

ISBN 0-88724-785-7

Table of Contents

Introduction

Building Phonemic Awareness with Poems

Rhythmic poems full of fun rhymes and alliteration are a natural motivator for teaching phonemic awareness to young children. They can be incorporated into any reading program to provide an exciting and interesting way to help develop the stages of phonemic awareness. Fun-filled poems are playful and help children gain the prerequisite skills needed for successful reading.

What Is Phonemic Awareness?

Before children can understand our written language, they must have a deep understanding of spoken language. They must learn how language and words work, as well as how to examine language so that they can manipulate and rearrange sounds to make new words. This knowledge of how language works is called phonemic awareness, and it is the foundation upon which many other reading skills are based.

Why Should Phonemic Awareness Be Taught?

Phonemic awareness is not something children are born with. It must be acquired before phonics can be taught successfully and should be an integral component of any beginning reading program. An emergent reader may have knowledge of letters and their names, but that is not enough. This familiarity with letters, combined with a multilevel phonemic awareness program, can bridge the critical gap between inadequate preparation for literacy and success in beginning reading.

Phonemic awareness begins with the awareness of spoken words, proceeds to syllables followed by onsets and rimes, and ends with individual sounds in a word. These stages of phonemic awareness can be incorporated into any current reading materials or programs so that they don't become an isolated skill.

What Makes These Poems Different from Other Poems?

These poems contain a sequential buildup of words, starting with high-frequency words most commonly used in beginning reading programs. Common beginning vocabulary words that are introduced in most reading programs are also incorporated. Each poem builds on the words from the previous poems, ensuring that there is frequent repetition of these important words. This repetition of vocabulary also provides ample opportunity for all children to be exposed over and over to the words they are learning in conjunction with whatever reading program is in use.

Each of the poems forms the basis for a lesson on key reading skills. As the poems is read, children learn how sound is related to print and that print has meaning. Using poetry to address phonemic awareness and early reading skills is a very effective way to expose children to a variety of prereading skills and activities.

There are 36 poems printed in black and white on removable pages, making it easy to reproduce copies for your whole class. Ten of the poems are also presented as full-color transparencies and can be projected on a wall or screen for the whole class to see.

A Note About Shared Reading

Shared reading is an instrumental tool for teaching children what reading is all about. Phonemic awareness can be taught in a shared reading experience, and gives the children a chance to look at pictures and print up close and to ask questions. In the shared reading of a poem, children are invited to participate regardless of their developmental levels. All children can be involved and are encouraged to join in reading with expression and fluency.

Ten of the poems are on transparencies and can be projected on a wall or screen for the whole class to see. The balance of the poems in this book can be written on a large piece of chart paper and placed on an easel or taped to the chalkboard. You could also copy a black-and-white example onto a sheet of transparency paper, color it with permanent markers, and then project it. However you choose to present the poems to the class, modeling by the teacher and child participation can occur simultaneously. This whole group setting gives students the opportunity to manipulate print in a concrete manner, allowing them to make choices and participate in a supportive environment. The poems encourage success and confidence.

In a shared reading setting, children learn the concepts of print, as well as many other beginning reading skills. When the poems are made available for children to revisit, they can practice independently and increase their core of high-frequency words, as well as build a solid base of beginning vocabulary words.

How Can the Poems Be Used in a Four-Blocks® Classroom?

Following are just a few examples of how the poems can be implemented into each block of the Four-Blocks® Literacy Model. Reproduce the black-and-white version of the poem the class will be working on, and provide a copy for each student.

The Guided Reading Block

1. On some days, the class does a shared reading of a poem where the teacher reads the poem first and then the children join in for frequent readings.

2. The poems can be tied into the children's other reading materials, reading skills being taught, other subjects, holidays, etc.

3. In the Guided Reading block, choral reading, echo reading, and shared reading are being modeled and practiced using the poems.

The Working with Words Block

1. Children exposed to shared reading with poems are learning automaticity of high-frequency words and vocabulary words used in the classroom.

2. With the transparencies or poetry charts, the teacher models how words work and how words are used to build sentences and stories. In this way, children learn to read and spell high-frequency words and to decode many other words as well.

3. Children learn to transfer this word knowledge to their own reading and writing.

4. Using the poems, children are introduced to many skills and activities that help them achieve the goal of learning how to work with words. They learn the concepts of print, look for patterns in words, learn about rhyming words, practice letter-sound discrimination, and learn how to decode many words and how to use them effectively to read and write. There are a myriad of ways to incorporate poems into Working with Words activities.

The Self-Selected Reading Block

1. Self-Selected Reading gives students a sense of control over their own learning because they get to choose what they want to read. Self-Selected Reading begins with the teacher reading aloud to the class from a wide range of literature, including the poems in this book.

2. At the end of every poetry lesson, the teacher places the poem chart in the poetry or reading center so that children can choose to read the poem independently during Self-Selected Reading. The easy poems are always left on display in order for the struggling readers to have a choice of poems to read on their own level.

3. The poems can be kept in a poetry notebook which gives the children another opportunity to select what they want to read.

The Writing Block

1. The Writing block begins with a short mini-lesson using the overhead or a large piece of chart paper. The teacher models a type of writing that the children will be able to achieve. She thinks out loud, and talks about what writers do. For example, after reading "Finnie Fish" she may draw a fish and write about a fish.

   Fish swim in water. Some swim in the ocean.
   Some swim in lakes. Some people have fish for pets.

2. Writing poetry is something young children can do. After reading a poem and talking about rhyming words, the teacher might choose to write a poem at writing time with the help of the class—this is shared writing! For example, after reading the poem "I Can Read," she might say some writers use rhyming words when they write. For her mini-lesson she might have them help her write a poem with rhyming words.

   Look at this book.
   It is about how to cook.
   Let's read it now.
   And find out how.

3. Sometimes the teacher models writing on "half and half" paper (blank space at the top and lines at the bottom). She draws a picture on top and writes on the lines below the picture. Drawing helps some children write. After reading the poem "Randy Raccoon," the teacher might draw a raccoon and then write about what the class knows about raccoons. Children interested in raccoons may want to continue writing about them when asked to do their own writing following the mini-lesson.

Helpful Ideas for Reading the Poems

Reading Wands
It is necessary to track the print as you read the rhyme with your students. There are many different types of wands that can be purchased from many of the educational catalogs. Dowels can also be purchased by the teacher and special effects can be glued on the end to go with a particular poem. For example, a paper kangaroo might be glued to the end of a dowel for use with "Katy Kangaroo" or "Jump and Hop." Let your imagination be your guide.

Word Windows
Windows can be used to focus on individual key words. These windows are easy to make by cutting a rectangle from the center of an index card, leaving enough room for a word to show through. A tongue depressor or craft stick can be glued to the back of the card for use as a handle. Word windows can also be purchased from school supply dealers.

Sticky String
A very successful tool to use for focusing on key words is sticky or waxed string, available from educational catalogs or teacher stores. Form a circle or an oval with the string and place it around a key word in the poem, pressing down so that it adheres to the paper or the transparency. Children love to come to the chart or overhead and find a word using this colorful string.

Guess the Covered Word
This activity helps children become aware of words that have been left out of a poem. You can use self-adhesive notes to cover key words that are being emphasized, such as rhyming words or vocabulary words. For example, in the poem "Can You Jump?" you might cover the word *jump* in the first line and the fourth line. As the poem is read, children will try to fill in the correct word. Uncover just the first letter and ask, "Were you right?" This continues until the whole word is uncovered. This activity is very helpful for practicing letter/sound discrimination and in making predictions about words.

Highlighting Words
After the poem has become familiar, give each child a copy of the poem. Reread it together and then ask the children to use a highlighter to highlight key words. For example, the teacher pronounces a rhyming word from the poem, and the children use their eyes and fingers to look for the word in their copies of the poem. When all have found and pointed to the word, they can then highlight it. Children also love to find and highlight punctuation marks, capital letters, titles, etc.

Pocket Chart Rhymes
The individual lines of a poem can be copied onto sentence strips. After the poem is familiar to the children, mix up the strips and put them in a pocket chart so the poem is out of order. Children can unscramble the poem and put it in the correct sequence. These strips are then put in a learning center for repeated practice.

Poetry Books
Children are given a copy of each poem to place into individual poetry books. Covers can be made of construction paper or tagboard and bound with fasteners, yarn, etc. Resealable plastic bags are also useful to store the poems in, are easy for children to handle, and can be used in the Self-Selected Reading block.

Words Used in the Poems

High-Frequency Words

The poems in this book contain many high-frequency words which you don't want children to have to decode while reading. As soon as possible, children should learn to read and write these words. When they do recognize and automatically spell them, all their attention is freed for decoding and spelling other words used less frequently. Thus, more attention can then be paid to processing the meaning of the story. Teaching the high-frequency words is not easy. Most of them are abstract words and have little or no meaning. Therefore, a good way to help children learn these words is by associating them with something meaningful. The poems contain many characters, words and ideas that have meaning for young children. As they reread the poems and participate in the suggested activities, the high-frequency words become a meaningful part of their everyday vocabulary. The more association and practice the children have with the words, the easier it will be to learn them. The high-frequency words are presented in a sequential order, ensuring their repetition and daily use.

High Frequency Words

a, about, all, am, and, around, away	me, my
big, brown	no, not
can, come	of, on, one, out
did, do	play, pull
eat	read, red, run
fast, find, for	say, see, show, sit, so, some, stop
get, go, good	take, that, the, there, this, thing, think, to,
have, he, here, him, his	today, try
I, if, in, is, it	up
jump, just	want, we, went, what, white, will, with
like, little, long, look	you

Lesson Format: A Sample Lesson

To help you understand how to use the poems in this book, the following suggestions and activities are presented in the framework of the Four-Blocks® Literacy Model. The activities have proved to be successful when implemented in a five-day format, but it is only one approach in which varied opportunities are given for all children to learn to read and write.

Guided Reading (Shared Reading of the Poem)
Day 1

1. Read the poem aloud to the children several times, tracking the print as you read. Challenge the children to listen carefully to the words, the rhythm, and the rhyme.

2. Ask the children to join in with you for rereadings of the poem. Read together in a variety of ways. (Choose one or two activities.)

   • Echo Read one sentence at a time. You read first and then pause and have the children repeat what you said (an echo). Children try to match the teacher's expression and phrasing.

   • Choral Read (read together in chorus). You may divide the room into two groups and take turns on every other line.

   • Choral Read and Echo Read in combination.

   • Recite-A-Rhyme. After children are familiar with the poem, say it again. This time, each time you come to a rhyming word, instead of saying it, cup a hand by your ear and have the children say the word in unison. Participation in this activity is a first step in preparing for "Rounding Up the Rhymes."

3. Act It Out

   Let the children take turns acting out the poem as it is read. They could pretend to be an animal in a poem hopping, jumping, running, etc. Let them be creative and use their imaginations.

Working with Words
Day 2 (Choose one or two activities.)

1. Flashlight Fun

   • Turn out the lights and play "Flashlight Fun." Say the poem together with the class. Then, repeat the phrase: "Flashlight, flashlight, oh so bright. Shine on a word with your light." Shine the flashlight on individual words for the class to read and chant. Since many of the words are repeated, shine the light on all the repeated words as well as the rhyming words. Proficient reading depends on the automatic ability to recognize frequently-used words, and this activity is a fun way to practice and reinforce this recognition of words.

   • As a follow-up to "Flashlight Fun," when the lights are turned back on, invite the children to come to the poetry chart and use one of the special wands to find the same words that were found with the flashlight. Children may also use a "word window" to focus on these individual words.

2. Be a Mind Reader

The teacher chooses one word from the poem to focus on, and gives five clues to the word. For example, here are five clues for the word *see* in "Barney Bear."

- It's one of the words in the poem.

- It has three letters.

- It begins with the letter *s*.

- It ends with the letter *e*.

- It's in the sentence, "_____ Barney Bear's brown hair!" This activity will help teach the difference between a letter and a word, an important concept about print for emergent readers.

3. Rounding Up the Rhymes

- Ask the children to identify two words that rhyme in the poem. Write them on index cards and put them in a pocket chart.

- Remind children that words that rhyme usually have the same spelling pattern.

- Invite a child to come and circle the spelling pattern in each word.

- Use these two words to read some other words. Write a word that rhymes and has the same spelling pattern as the "rounded up pair." Put it under the two rhyming words and then read all three words. Add more words as time allows.

Self-Selected Reading
Day 3 (Choose one or two activities.)

1. Teacher Read-Aloud

- Read aloud from a variety of literature and instructional-level materials. Use easy books, challenging books, Dr. Seuss books, rhyming books, and informational books.

- In Self-Selected Reading, children get to choose what they want to read; therefore, it is important for the teacher to model reading to the children and provide many different kinds of grade-level reading materials. There should be daily read-alouds and time for reading books of their own choice.

- After reading and sharing a poem about a kangaroo, dog, pig, etc., the teacher can read a selection of books about other animals to whet their appetites.

Following are only a few of the animal books that could be read aloud for this purpose.

Animals at Night by Sharon Peters (Troll Communications, 1983).

Good-Night, Owl! by Pat Hutchins (Aladdin Paperbacks, 1990).

Golden Bear by Ruth Young (Puffin, 1994).

It's Not Easy Being a Bunny by Marilyn Sadler (Random House, 1983).

Zoo-Looking by Mem Fox (Mondo Publishing, 1996).

Owl at Home by Arnold Lobel (HarperCollins Children's Books, 1982).

Over in the Meadow by Paul Galdone (Simon & Schuster Children's, 1991).

Those Can-Do Pigs by David McPhail (Penguin Putnam Books for Young Readers, 1999).

Puffins Climb, Penguins Rhyme by Bruce McMillan (Harcourt, 2001).

Is Your Mama a Llama? by Deborah Guarino (Scholastic, Inc., 1997).

Possum Come A-Knockin' by Nancy Van Laan (Alfred A. Knopf, 1992).

Jesse Bear, What Will You Wear? by Nancy Carlstrom (Simon & Schuster Children's, 1996).

- The teacher adds these books to the appropriate center so the children can read and look at them during Self-Selected Reading.

2. Centers

- Centers are provided in the classroom so that the children may read from a variety of sources. Centers could be set up in many different ways and may include the following: big book center, magazine center, class-authored book center, science center, taped book read-along center, and poetry center.

- Copies of the poems are put in the poetry center, along with envelopes containing cut-up sentences taken from the poems. They are used for matching and rebuilding.

- The teacher could also have a small group reading center, with as many as five children included. This "coaching group" may include different children for different reasons on different days. The teacher will be able to check up on how struggling children are applying strategies and can coach them as needed.

- The teacher makes one copy of the poem for each child. It is added to the child's poetry notebook, resealable plastic bag, or whatever is used for storing familiar books or poems.

Writing
Day 4

1. Mini-Lesson – Teacher Writing

Procedure

- The teacher begins the mini-lesson by putting a piece of story paper on the board. "Today I am going to write about the lizard from our poem that we shared. Let's see if I can think of why it is time for the lizard to run." The teacher then writes a simple sentence or two the first time, modeling how to look at the Word Wall for words she knows are there and stretching out other words. The teacher may draw a picture that goes with the story.

- Next, the children do their writing. Some children may draw first and just write their names. Others write a few words and draw. Some write a whole sentence. The teacher goes around and encourages the students, but she does not spell words. Instead, she helps the child stretch the word out and write some letters. After 10-15 minutes, the teacher gathers the children together to share their stories, responding positively to what they share.

- Children in early first grade like to pretend they can write. They do this by combining drawing along with some circle/line, letter-like forms, some letters and a few words, which sometimes are copied from a book, a sign, or picture. The children like to read what they have written. This "driting" could also begin in the Writing Block, since many children may not have done driting at home or in kindergarten.

Review of the Poem
Day 5

The teacher may use this day for children to review the poem for the week. Following are just a few of the ways in which this can be done.

- Highlighting Words (For more information on Highlighting Words, see page 7.)

  Children use their individual copies of the poem to find key words, punctuation marks, titles, etc., as the teacher pronounces them.

- Reading Wands in the Poetry Center (For more information on Reading Wands, see page 7.)

  Children use wands to track and read the poetry charts which have been placed in the center for Self-Selected Reading.

- Pocket Chart Rhymes (For more information on Pocket Chart Rhymes, see page 7.)

  Children can unscramble the poem and put it in the correct order.

- Partner Read

  Children may pair up and read a poem to a partner or "buddy." Older children can also be used to listen to them read.

- Homework

  Copies of the poems may be sent home with the children so that they may share their success with family members.

Barney Bear

Barney Bear, Barney Bear,
I like Barney Bear.
See Barney Bear.
See Barney Bear.
See Barney Bear's brown hair!

Clancy Cat

This is Clancy the cat.

He likes to jump and hop.

He likes to play with Sally's ball.

Stop, Clancy, stop!

Digger Dog

Digger can jump.

Digger can hop.

Digger can play, play, play.

Jump, Digger, jump!

Hop, Digger, hop!

Jump and hop today.

Finnie Fish

I like my little pet.
His name is Finnie Fish.
He likes to swim around,
In a teeny, tiny dish!

Grumpy Goat

Grump, grump, Grumpy Goat,

Wears a long, white coat.

He chews on hay.

He chews on grass.

He chews and chews all day.

Harry Hippo

Hip, hip, hip-hip hooray,
Harry Hippo swims all day.
Swim, swim here.
Swim, swim there.
Harry Hippo swims
everywhere!

Jiffy Jet

Jiffy is a great big jet.
He likes to fly up high.
See him fly way up, up, up,
Up to the big blue sky!

Katy Kangaroo

Katy Kangaroo lives in a pouch.

She gets to take a ride.

Oh, what fun it is to play.

Get down and hide, hide, hide.

Lizzie Lizard

Lizzie Lizard likes to sit
In the hot, hot sun.
Hurry, hurry, hurry up.
It is time to run!

Monster Mouse

Monster Mouse
Lives in my house,
In a big, big box.
He likes to munch, munch,
Munch on cheese,
And tries to eat my socks!

22

Naughty Nick

Here is a boy. His name is Nick.

He likes to kick, kick, kick.

He kicks the dog.

He kicks the cat.

His brother calls him Nick the brat.

Penny Penguin

Hurry, hurry, little penguin,
Playing in the snow.
Will you come and play with me?
I hope you won't say no!

24

Quiet Quail

Can you find the quiet quail
Sitting in the sun?
Can you find his little brown tail?
He likes to run and run and run.

Randy Raccoon

Randy's home is in a tree.

He likes to sleep all day.

It is time to wake him up.

"Wake up, so we can play!"

Sammy Seal

Sammy's waiting for his fish.
He will sit and wait and wait.
"Hurry, hurry, hurry up.
I want something on my plate!"

Tommy Tiger

A tiger is a big, big cat.

He loves to race and run.

Race and run. Race and run.

Running in the sun!

Vinny Vulture

Vinny likes to sit and wait
For something good to eat.
Hurry, hurry, it is time
To go and find a treat!

Wally Walrus

Wally Wally Walrus,
I see you.
Wally Wally Walrus,
Peekaboo!
Wally Wally Walrus,
I like you.
Wally Wally Walrus
Is my friend, too.

Yakky Yak

Yakky Yak is big.

Yakky Yak is strong.

Yakky Yak has hair.

His hair is way too long!

Zeke Zebra

Zeke the Zebra
Lives in the zoo.
He likes to follow the vet.
Do you have a friend for me?
I want him for a pet.

32

Read Me a Book

Read me a book.

Read me a book.

Read me a book today.

Can you read?

Can you read?

We can read and play.

Jump and Hop

Jump, jump, jump, jump, jump.

Hop, hop, hop, hop, hop.

Jump and hop.

Jump and hop.

Jump and hop up to the top.

I Can Read

I can read. I can read.
I can read a book.
I will read. I will read.
Will you look, look, look?

Can You Jump and Hop?

See me jump.

See me jump.

See me jump and hop.

Can you jump?

Can you hop?

Try to stop, stop, stop!

Put the Ball In

Put it in.

Put it in.

Put the big ball in.

You can try.

You can try.

You can try to win!

37

You Can Do It

Did you do it?

Did you do it?

Did you hop, hop, hop?

You can do it.

You can do it.

Do not stop, stop, stop!

Finish

Can You?

Can you jump?

Can you hop?

Can you swim like me?

I can jump.

I can hop.

I can swim. Come see!

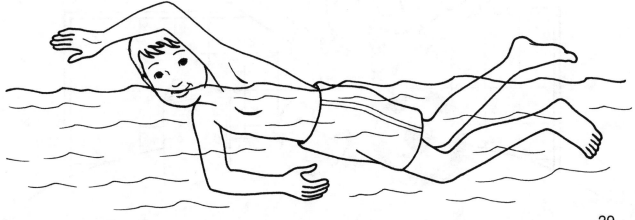

I Will Show You

I got a ball.

I got a duck.

I got a little book.

I will show you.

I will show you.

I will show you. Look!

I Can Do It

I can read a book.

I can try to cook.

I can swim in a lake.

And, I can try to bake.

I can jump and hop.

I can try to mop.

I can hit the ball.

And, I can do it all.

To the Lake

I went to the lake.

I went to swim.

I went to the lake to swim with Tim.

I went to the tree.

I went to sit.

I went to the tree to sit with Kit.

Cannot

A pig cannot bark.
A duck cannot moo.
A dog cannot quack.
And, a frog cannot coo.

Run About

Run about, run about,

Run about the trees.

Race and run.

Race and run.

Will you wait for me?

Little Things

I like little boats.

I like little ducks.

I like little trains.

I like little trucks.

I like so many little things:

Frogs and books and pretty rings,

And little birds that sing!

I Can Pull

I can pull a wagon.

I can pull a duck.

I can pull a little train.

And, I can pull a truck.

The Big Red Train

I like to ride on my big red train.

I like to ride in the rain, rain, rain.

See me race and go so fast.

I will win and not be last.

I sit up on the engine so tall.

Up so high, I see it all.

I'm a Little Snowman

I'm a little snowman
Short and fat.
Here are my buttons,
Here is my hat.
When the sun comes out,
I cannot play.
Slowly, I just melt away.